D1082919

Don't Go Up a Windmill

Poems by
Steve Rideout

Illustrated by
Greg Fairholm, pages 5-36
Jenine Kelly, pages 37-61
Anton Dimov, pages 62-89

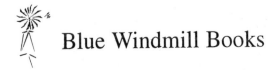 Blue Windmill Books

DON'T GO UP A WINDMILL

Blue Windmill Books
PO Box 194
Blue Springs, MO 64013

For Steve Rideout Author Program booking write
Blue Windmill Books or windmill@flash.net

Watch for steverideout.com

ISBN 0-9670157-0-7
ISBN 0-9670157-1-5 (lib.bdg.)

Forward

Steve Rideout believes in what he is doing - - delighting audiences and stirring up interest in reading and writing. And he's brave. I applaud his courage for talking openly about the trauma-laden dilemma of being a boy Ladybug or a girl Daddy Longlegs. He is also a gentleman who staunchly defends old-time virtues such as giving the teacher an apple, albeit one with a tiny flaw. Reading Rideout is simply a good idea. I recommend that you begin immediately.

David Harrison
Award winning author of forty-five children's books

To Ann, Sarah, Ben, and Abbey

APPLE FOR MY TEACHER

I'm taking an apple to my favorite teacher,
But it looks so juicy and red.
There may be a chance that this apple won't reach'er,
'Cause I think I might eat it instead.

Well, Mom says to eat stuff that's healthy for me,
So eating it would be OK.
I know if I'd ask her that she would agree,
I could bring one to school next Monday.

What's this, there's a hole with a worm sticking out!
Eating that wouldn't be cool.
My discov'ry has taken away any doubt.
Yes, I must take this apple to school.

Pleasing my teacher is my only goal,
So eating it wouldn't be right.
I hope that she doesn't discover the hole,
'Til after she takes a big bite!

APRIL 15

Beware my friend, the fifteenth day,
The fourth month from the first.
That is the day that some may say,
Could be by far your worst.

Abe Lincoln could attest to that,
For while at the theater,
A bullet that shot through his hat,
Sent him to his Creator.

A ship was dubbed "unsinkable."
We all know the Titanic.
Icebergs did the unthinkable,
Sank it in the Atlantic.

The infamy continues on,
A happening that hacks us.
And that's why all our money's gone,
'Cause folks must pay their taxes.

BORED

I'm sitting in my class.
I wish the time would pass,
MUCH FASTER!

BASEBALL SURPRISE

I finally made the Lions.
A goal for which I've strived.
For years I have been tryin',
I finally have arrived.

I got my uniform,
And took it from the box.
There's shirts for cold and warm,
With stirrups, hat, and socks.

I put it on with such a fling,
I got all suited up.
And then I noticed one more thing,
I think it's called a cup.

I've heard it mentioned once or twice,
But don't know how it's used.
It doesn't look so awful nice.
I think I am confused.

I talked to Dad, "I can't believe,
I have to wear it where!"
It wasn't easy to conceive,
I had to put it there!

I'm told George Brett and Willie Mays,
Have worn them with no strife.
And Dad says there will be some days,
That it may save my life.

BIG YELLOW TORPEDO

The car won't start we've tried and tried.
Agony! Defeat! Oh
No! That means I'm forced to ride
The big yellow torpedo.

I hate riding the bus to school.
It's awful when I do.
I know I'll feel just like a fool.
It really is a zoo.

Kids who ride the bus are dumb.
I hope no one will see me.
Maybe a limousine will come,
And from this torture free me.

Sit in the back, I'll
bounce and shake
With all the rowdy bands.
And if I do I'll
surely take
My life in my
own hands.

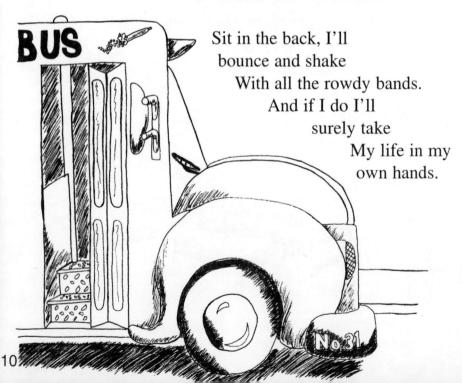

Up in the front the kids are found
Who really are too formal.
So to the middle I am bound,
For they're closer to the normal.

What's this? I can't believe it now.
I know this cannot be.
Well, I'm about to have a cow,
'Cause my best friend I see.

"I didn't know you rode the bus.
You've not told me," I shouted.
"Stop causing a humongous fuss.
You didn't ask," he spouted.

Riding the bus, it is not great,
But it is kind of cool.
I'll have to re-evaluate
When I get to high school.

Tomorrow when I ride the big yellow torpedo,
I won't have to go incognito.

DINOSAUR

I'd love to have a dinosaur.
Bet he'd not make it through the door.
Into the shower he'd not fit,
And that would make him stink a bit.
I couldn't get him tons of food,
So he'd be in an awful mood.
We'd have to keep him in the yard,
And that would make things much too hard.
A dinosaur is a great pet.
But I can tell you what, I bet
I know just what my mom would say.
"You can't have it. Take it away!"
So if I can't I'll rave and rant,
And maybe get an elephant.

DON'T GO UP A WINDMILL

I know that it's been said,
Or at least I think I've read.
Perhaps I heard it on the intercom.
Yes, don't you ever go up on a windmill without Mom.

Going up a windmill could bring hazards to your health.
If you should fall you'd prob'ly loose your life,
   perhaps your wealth.
    Bad things can happen to you when
      your mom is not around.
        She must be there to see you get back safely to the ground!

   If going up a windmill is an every day occurrence.
     You must be very, very sure that you have good insurance.
           Your best insurance policy is
           someone you call Mom.
           If she's not there your life
           may never last until the prom.

           I'll shout it from the
              rooftops; I will
              light a cherry bomb.
           But just promise that
           you won't go up a
             windmill without Mom.

DREAMING

When it's late at night
And dreams get in your head,
You may die of fright
Or even wet the bed.

Anything can be
In your dreams so vivid.
Dreams can make you happy,
Or sad, or even livid.

You could dream you're stressed
While others have good mood.
Folks may be fully dressed,
And you'd be in the nude!

In dreams some may be bad,
Some others may be scary.
And more may make you glad,
Like Curly, Moe, and Larry!

I know that dreams can be
So scary or so weird.
Some night I just might see
My grandma with a beard!

EPIDERMIS IS SHOWIN'

I was in the lunchroom with all my best friends.
Think we were discussing my new contact lens.
My friends were all happy, and my heart was glowin'.
Then someone said my epidermis was showin'.

I could have disappeared right through the wall,
For I never knew epidermis at all.
The sound of it was just as strange as can be,
And all of my friends were now staring at me.

I wanted to look but I dared not stare down,
For fear I'd be so shocked at what I had found.
Embarrassment just got the better of me,
So I took a look down 'cause I just had to see.

Alas, when I looked there my heart did not stop.
The flag on my zipper was up at the top.
I felt not a rip when I checked out my rear.
They started to laugh, and that shot up my fear.

They said, "Don't get
mad now it's only a joke.
We never get mad when
at us fun you poke."
I realized right then
what a fool I had been,
When they said
epidermis was only my
skin!

EYES

I eyed her eyes and she eyed mine,
And she was lookin' mighty fine.
But then I noticed something weird.
It wasn't like she had a beard.
But something didn't seem just right,
That very warm and starry night.
And then it finally came to me.
I had two eyes, but she had three!

"F"

An F on a test is not really so bad,
Until you go home and tell Mother and Dad.
I guess that Miss Quigley just had a bad day,
But all my friends passed it, or that's what they say.

That just isn't fair, how come they passed the test?
I know that I did do my dead level best!
I studied real hard for at least fifteen minutes
And put every bit of my heart and soul in it.

I may have done well if I'd studied some better.
I would have received a more popular letter.
I'll study next time so my grade I'll be turnin',
So people won't think that I ain't had no learnin'.

P.S. My dad didn't yell
or ban me from the yard,
So maybe I won't have
to study "that" hard.

I GOTTA GO

I'm sittin' at my desk, and I am gettin' kinda wiggley.
I'm doin' all I can to get attention from Miss Quigley.
She has to know the possibility of pending doom.
Cause, oh... do I have to go to the bathroom!

"You're always getting out of class,"
Is what Miss Quigley said.
I said, "If you don't let me go, I prob'ly will be dead."
"I know what you will do," she said.
"You'll go in there and groom.
So, no...
You can't go to the bathroom!"

"You've had your two this week,
that's all you get, that is the rule.
And if I let you go
I'll have to keep you after school."
I'm destined to just sit in class
And put up with the gloom.
I have to wait another week...
To go to the bathroom!

I'D BETTER LIKE BEING A KID

My mom and dad say don't complain about age,
But I am too young to make minimum wage.

They say they would love to go back to their youth.
Do you really think they are telling the truth?

Mom says, "It's not nearly as fun when you're older."
"But you don't have zits and get grounded," I told'er!

"I'd take a few zits for more hair any day,"
My dad said, while rubbing his back with Bengay.

Mom said, "I've got wrinkles, gray hair, and eye bags,
And Dad's muscle tone is now turning to sags!"

I better like being a kid if I'm smart.
'Cause when I get older,
I may fall apart!

LITTLE TURTLE

Little turtle in the road
Don't you know you're not a toad?
Many cars will swerve and sway,
But you can't jump out of the way.

Little turtle in the street
On your legs you are not fleet.
Pick-up trucks will whiz and dart,
And you'll end up like modern art!

Little turtle on the highway
Unlike a bird you cannot fly away.
Eighteen wheelers rumble by,
And you'll be squashed like pumpkin pie.

MAY I HAVE YOUR ATTENTION

There's kids at the door getting ready for lunch.
We're standing there talking in kind of a bunch.
It suddenly happened the reason is clear,
Why Ben stuck his finger in Miss Quigley's ear.

Miss Quigley said, "Stop that, Ben, what are you doing?"
Just what kind of nonsense could you be pursuing?
She went right on talking to others I s'pose,
So Ben's index finger went right up her nose.

She said, "Stop that now 'fore you get a detention!"
He answered, "I'm trying to get your attention!"
Miss Quigley said, "Patience must first be displayed.
Keep fingers away or I'll be more dismayed."

Now should you be wanting your teacher's attention,
There are a few things that I think I should mention.
You must keep your fingers away from her nose,
Or at least you should wait
until after she blows.

MY NOSE

Why is my nose so dog gone big?
I ought to hide it with a wig!

I know it isn't a mirage.
Looks more like a two-car garage!

I kind of like it, for you see,
It takes in air, and air is free!

PIANO LESSONS

I just hate piano lessons.
My coordination's lacking.
If I mess up my next session,
Mrs. Sharp might send me packing.

When my fingers start a'playin'
Bach or Beethoven, I stink.
I had better start a'prayin'
'Fore they send me to a shrink.

My hands are both retarded,
They just hit all the wrong keys.
It sounds as if I've started
Playing keyboard with my knees.

I don't want to upset'er,
So I won't quit, I suppose.
If my fingers don't do better,
I might try to use my toes!

NOTE

Miss Quigley with a note caught me,
Now in my seat I cower.
I'm 'fraid my consequence will be
A darn detention hour.

Why does she always just catch me?
I'm not the only one.
My friends all do it, can't she see?
She ruins all my fun.

I said, "All of the class has notes,
But you just pick on me."
After her eyes began to float
Miss Quigley said, "Guilty!"

"Now that you've got us all off track
There's something I should mention.
Because you're always talking back,
You've got in-school detention."

I tried to yell, nothing came out,
My insides started fumin'.
Miss Quigley is beyond a doubt
The world's most vicious human.

I'm stuck with in-school for three days.
My life has just been wrecked.
To top it off my dad will say,
"You're grounded," I suspect.

I finally did myself compose,
But I am not a quitter.
I said, "Miss Quigley, you don't s'pose
That you would reconsider?"

25

That's when a hush went through the air.
They not believed I'd asked'r.
She ran her fingers through her hair
And started talking faster.

"I reached the verdict hastily.
I'll give you what you seek.
"Forget the three days ISD
For now you have a week."

"A week, you can't do that!" I said,
"That really isn't fair."
That's when I realized I was dead
And slunk into my chair.

Her body started shakin',
Her face was red no doubt.
I knew she wasn't fakin'
When she finally yelled, "Get out!"

That's how I got in this big mess.
I'm in the office now.
You think it'd help if I confess?
I really don't know how.

I'm sitting in a deep morass.
My days they may be few.
I prob'ly won't get back to class
Until I'm thirty-two.

PIGEON

Would anyone like to be a pigeon?
I've no desire, no not a smidgen.

How about a roadrunner?
That could be a lot funner.

I'd like to be an eagle.
Ya think it would be legal?

You want to be a cow bird?
That's the weirdest thing I've heard.

Would you consider a crow?
NO!

I think I'll be a wren.
Will I be happy then?

I'll just stay little ole me,
For I've no choice, you see.

TWO BITS

Two bits, four bits,
Six bits, a dollar,
If you're in a library
Stand up and holler!

[Warning: The librarian has determined that
this could be hazardous to your health]

SCHOOL BULLY

I am the school bully and I'll punch you in the face,
Or stuff you in a locker and not even leave a trace.
Your stomach is my target, and your head will be my drum.
That's all that I can do because I really am so dumb.

I can't succeed at readin', writin', or arithmetic,
And comin' up with answers use'ly I'm not very quick.
I'll never catch a ball, and I will never win a race,
But I have found success at punchin' people in the face.

So don't be givin' me no lip or any other stuff.
I'm not a rocket scientist, but I am pretty tough.
Just don't be comin' close to me, just stay out of my space.
For I'm the school bully, and I'll punch you in the face.

There is no honor student sticker on my mother's car.
And when I tried to steal one once, I didn't get too far.
My dad got him a sticker so I wouldn't feel disgrace.
His pick-up says I punched your honor student
in the face.

SODABURP

Some folks call it soda.
Some folks call it pop.
It makes me burp so loud,
I wish that I could stop!

SILENT LETTERS

Why does the opossum have an O
At the beginning of his name?
Without the O, does not he know
He's a'possum just the same?

Pneumonia starts with P, it's true.
Why doesn't it start with N?
If it starts with cough or flu,
You really are sick then.

Often is a curious word.
Most folks don't say the T.
A drink with jam and bread, I've heard,
Some tea sounds good to me.

So what a tricky thing to do,
To put an L in salmon.
But even drowned in barbecue,
I'd only eat'em in famine.

Knowledge is the thing they say
That tends to make us smarter.
But must they start it with a K
To make it even harder?

I know a tricky one to be,
The state of Illinois "S"?
And even when in Tennessee,
The S will still annoy us.

If K-N-I-F-E spells knife,
Or so I have been told,
I'll ask why there's no K in life,
If I may be so bold.

Does aardvark have a silent A?
A double A is worst.
And with two A's it's hard to say
If the silent one's second or first?

While searching, I, for escargot,
I knew not the silent T.
And then I found it's snails you know,
Alas, they're not for me.

What would this new discussion be,
Without the G in gnu?
You knew that gnu's not new to me,
And the new gnu you knew knew it too.

SPOONERISMS

My mother always told me I should never nick my pose.
She said don't do it as a kid, and 'specially when I grows.

Mama also taught me shy my toos and flip my zy.
I'd better learn the latter or someone might say, "Oh my."

Some other good advice from Mom to never ratch my screar.
If someone would observe that act how strangely I'd appear.

As I got older Mama said to always flean my case,
For if I didn't do that I'd have pimples peverylace.

Mama always had me put my lapkin in my nap,
And after lunch you know she'd always have me nake a tap.

If Cinderella was her kid, I know advice she'd slip'er.
She'd say get home on time so you won't have to "slop your
dripper."

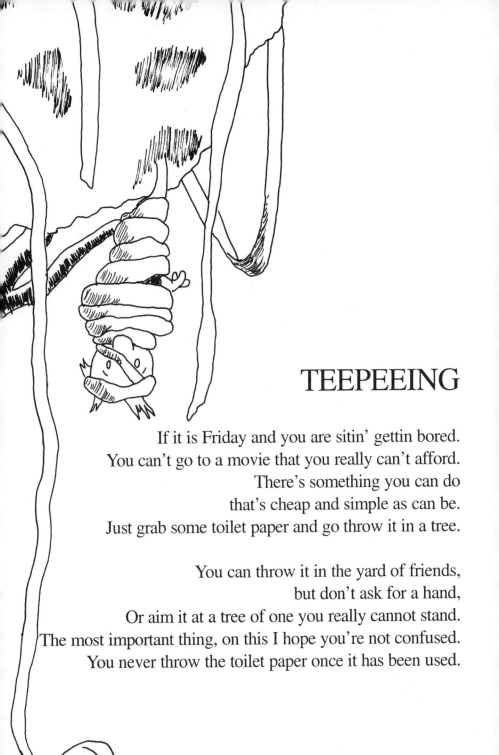

TEEPEEING

If it is Friday and you are sitin' gettin bored.
You can't go to a movie that you really can't afford.
There's something you can do
that's cheap and simple as can be.
Just grab some toilet paper and go throw it in a tree.

You can throw it in the yard of friends,
but don't ask for a hand,
Or aim it at a tree of one you really cannot stand.
The most important thing, on this I hope you're not confused.
You never throw the toilet paper once it has been used.

TWISTER

Twister, twister, twister, twister,
I can tell you one thing mister.
I just saw one yesterday.
Almost blew my house away.

Cyclone, cyclone, cyclone, cyclone,
Please don't leave me here alone.
Better find a place to hide,
'Fore it takes me for a ride.

Tornado, tornado, tornado, tornado.
I am getting more afraid. Oh,
Micro winds with violent breezes,
Carry off just what they pleases.

POISON IVY

I sat in poison ivy once.
I didn't know it then.
So do you think I am a dunce?
I won't do it again.

I started itching, turning red
In several private places.
It made me wish that I were dead,
Because of social graces.

'Cause there are places you can't itch
When you're with other folks.
And if they see you scratch or twitch
You're subject of their jokes.

I doused myself with calamine,
My patience wearing thin.
Just when I thought it's feelin' fine,
I'd start to itch again!

The itching finally did subside,
I can walk, run, and dance.
And if again I go outside,
I'll wear ten pairs of pants.

ANN OF SEVENTH HOUR

I'm sitting in my seventh hour,
Staring at her face, a flower.
But she will never notice me,
To her I'm just a tiny flea.

Annie is her glorious name.
Her beauty could a lion tame.
But Annie never looks my way.
She won't give me the time of day.

Oh, what a couple we could make.
To all the parties I would take,
Annie, my pretty little queen.
In the right places, we'd be seen.

I'd treat her just like royalty,
And in my presence she would see
Accompanying any other,
Would be like going out with her brother.

"Oh yes, Miss Quigley, I'm on task.
Why it's so funny you should ask,
For on your class I'm contemplating,
And on my work I'm concentrating."

"No, not a girl would but distract me."
I tried to say matter of factly.
"My mind to girls does never stray."
Cracks in my voice gave me away.

What happened next I can't explain,
For in my heart arose a pain.
But that's when Annie smiled at me,
And pain evolved to ecstasy!

CARROTS

I eat so many carrots,
That you'd think I was a rabbit.
My mom says they are good for me,
But I don't care, dag nabbit!
I eat 'em 'cause I like 'em,
And I've gotten in the habit.
You'd better watch your carrot;
If you don't I just might grab it!

CATS

In this square I'll show
All the good I know
About cats.

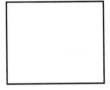

And that's that.
SKAT!

ELEANOR GIGGLE

Eleanor Giggle
Had a funny wiggle.
She swayed from side to side.
She tried to amend it,
But she couldn't end it,
No matter how hard she tried.

She went to the doctor,
But he merely walked 'er
Across the room and back.
He said, "Lose some weight,
Or you'll have a date
With an early heart attack."

"You're big as a house,
And I may be a louse,
But I'm sorry to be blunt.
You're turning gray,
And the way you sway,
You look like an elephant."

She said, "I don't s'pose,
That you've noticed my nose.
It hangs down to my feet.
You are getting frail,
If you've not seen my tail.
Your exam is not complete!"

Now I don't want to vex you,
Or even perplex you.
This may come as sort of a shock.
But since my birth,
Here on this earth,
I have been an elephant, Doc!"

FILIBUSTER

I didn't get my homework done
It did me truly fluster.
I'll have to ask hour number one
To start a filibuster.

We could read a shopping list
Or from Sports Illustrated.
They'd cover up the work I missed,
And I would be elated.

I'll take the want add section
And the World Book of "D".
They will provide protection
Keep Miss Quigley's mind off me.

That's what the
congressmen will do
So votes cannot be taken.
It works for them,
why not me too?
There is no law
I am breakin'.

If this won't work
what shall I do?
I'll be down in the dumps.
I'd better try
plan number two;
Stay home,
and fake the mumps.

FIREFLY

A firefly
Came flying by.
I heard him say oh me, oh my,
I'm having trouble with my light.
It used to be so very bright,
But there is something just not right.
I cannot turn it on!
I guess my spark is gone.
It used to light from dusk to dawn,
But this is a strange quirk.
My light, it just won't work.
Oh no! I'm feeling like a jerk.
My feelings might amuse,
But I won't sing the blues,
For I have just discovered that
I've only blown a fuse!

FOOTBALL PIE

Henry Ant played quarterback on Mrs. Doolap's pie.
As he did he took a bite, and Henry thought mmmm-my!

He wasn't a John Elway, all his passes were not caught.
But Henry didn't mind for there'd be better days, he thought.

Some day he'll throw his passes, and they all will be complete.
And when he wins the Super Bowl that will be pretty neat.

But Mrs. Doolap spotted him, and sprang up to her feet.
She hit him with a rolling pin, now Henry's incomplete!

FRECKLES

I know there are kids who have freckly faces,
But I seem to get them all over my places.

They grow up my arms, down my legs, on my toes,
And I have a bumper crop right on my nose.

Most grownups will say that they make me look handsome.
They ought to be banished, at least held for ransom.

I do have a spot there are no freckles there.
I never have seen them
in my underwear.

I've just about had it.
My brain's on the loose.
I wish you could find me
some un-freckle juice.

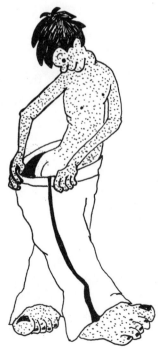

GIGGLY GIRLS

You know that girls giggle so.
I cannot tell you why.
It doesn't matter where they go.
They'll giggle 'til they die.

They giggle when they're in the yard
At a tree, a cat, a bunny.
But I do find it pretty hard
To see just what's so funny.

They giggle when they're in a group,
And when they're all alone.
They even giggle eating soup,
And 'specially on the phone.

They giggle nearly night and day.
    It seems to bring them joys.
        But they are happiest they say
            When giggling at boys.

HEAVEN SENT

Mom says God sent my baby brother dear,
When I was at the tender age of seven.
It seems to me the reason's very clear.
He was so bad they kicked him out of heaven.

IN THE FALL

In the fall, we have a ball,
Jumping in the leaves and all.
But it's not fair, we have to rake.
Why do they fall for heaven's sake?

IN THE WINTER

In the winter it is cold.
Not fit for man nor beast, I'm told.
Icicles hanging from the gutter,
Have to thaw out my little brudder.
I think it might be wise of I
To fly south like the butterfly.

IN THE SPRING

In the spring,
The flowers blossom,
The birdies sing,
They're sounding awesome.
My winter boots,
Away I threw'm.
Last summer's suits,
I have outgrew'm

IN THE SUMMER

In the summer, it's a bummer.
We don't get to go to school.
Playing all day's just not right,
Neither's staying up all night.
If you believe this,
You're a fool!

IN THE LIBRARY

I went to the library to take a look.
I really didn't want to check out a book,
But this one just jumped out at me,
This very book of poetry.
Oh gross!
You don't suppose
It's happening to you too?
What are you going to do?
Why don't you read it now, you kid?
Oh, since you're here, I guess you did.

JARED LEAR

Jared Lear
Lost his rear.
He couldn't find it anywhear.
It was there but he couldn't find it,
So the doctor realigned it.
It's crooked now, but he don't mind it!

JUST A DUCK

I want to be an eagle,
But I'm just a little duck.
I want to soar the mountain heights,
Guess I am out of luck.

Gliding through the clouds all day,
Is always in my dreams.
I guess I'll have to settle,
For my little pond, it seems.

Oh, I can fly,
It isn't hard to get up in the air.
But when an eagle flaps his wings,
He does it with such flair.

I want to be important,
Yes, I want to be top dog.
But I am just a little duck,
Just sitting on a log.

An eagle's flight is elegant,
He stands for what is strong.
And when I try to imitate,
I always get it wrong.

To have the strength of eagle claws,
That really would be neat.
But that is pretty difficult,
When you're born with webbed feet.

My mom says to stop dreaming
And to get my life in order.
But I would like to have my face
On the back of every quarter.

I must look on the bright side,
For there's one thing I'm not called.
You see, unlike the eagle,
here's no duck that has gone bald!

MY DOG

My dog, she is a carnivore,
But that's not all that she's good for.
She'll snarf down carrots, broccoli,
And other stuff that's not for me!

At meals she sits down at my feet,
And what I don't like she will eat.
My mom thinks I am eating it.
If she finds out she'll have a fit!

My radishes and cauliflower,
She'll eat them all at dinner hour.
Her favorite is my whole wheat bread.
If I get caught, I will be dead!

RINGO

I know a guy named Ringo,
Who thinks he's a flamingo.
He isn't even pink!
I think he needs a shrink!
He has no wings,
Or other things,
To prove he is a bird.
Golly, how absurd.

SCHOOL FOOD

If my mom makes me eat in the school cafeteria,
I'll just run away and end up in Siberia.
Or maybe I'll cry till the tears run down my back,
And then I'll stay home with a case of back-tear-ia!

SCHOOL PRAYER

My good friend Mantis got kicked out of school the other day.
For as you know, my friend the praying mantis likes to pray.
He folded up his hands, and then he slowly bowed his head.
"Hey Mantis, you are not allowed to pray," our teacher said.

You cannot bow your head,
you must sit straight like all the rest.
But then my friend the mantis said, "I'm going to take a test!
When I'm about to undertake a task that's what I do.
You've always taught us that we live in freedom, is that true?"

"Well, yes," the teacher said,
"The Pilgrims came here for that reason.
They gave thanksgiving and they celebrated harvest season."
Then Mantis said, "Excuse me, if it's all the same to you.
I'm doing what I know is best and not what others do."

"I'm gonna pray at anytime just when I feel the need.
Not you nor anybody else has rights to intercede.
I know what's going on across
this nation. I'm no fool.
Where there are teachers
giving tests,
there will be
prayer in school!"

SHOPPING SPREE

Sarah went on a shopping spree,
'Cause she was in a tither.
When she returned just after three,
The whole darn store was with'er!

SKUNK

I met a skunk who thunk he stunk,
I didn't think he might.
I scared that skunk who thunk he stunk,
That wasn't very bright.
I smelled the skunk who thunk he stunk,
And guess what, he was right!

ABBEY

When I first walk into the house,
If I am quiet as a mouse,
Or if I'm noisy as a hog,
She'll come to me, my faithful dog.

With happy whines my ears she blesses,
And with her tongue my nose caresses.
That's when she'll cuddle by my knee,
And we'll just sit, Abbey and me.

Should clouds bring snow, or cold, or rain,
She'll do her duty, not complain.
But call her in, and if she's wet,
She'll be a wild and woolly pet.

When I should chance to throw a ball,
She'll bring it back, slobber and all.
Her favorite toy is her balloony.
It revs her up and makes her loony.

If for some reason I am sad,
She'll make my sad seem not so bad.
And if a tear runs down my face,
She'll lick it off in record pace.

Sometimes at night if dreams bring fear,
Won't be afraid, for she is near.
She will be faithful 'til the end.
Abbey's a true and trusted friend.

Your cat does this is what you say?
AIN'T NO WAY!

BEANS

If I had my choice of food,
I prob'ly would choose beans.
When I eat them I am rude.
I sing beneath my jeans!

If it happens at school
I get plenty of stares
Miss Quigley says,
"Stop playing musical chairs!"

I cannot be quiet!
I will not deny it!
I hope I can stop,
So I won't cause a riot!

BLACK WIDOW

Well, a spider named Matilda,
Said, "To see you I am thrilled'a.
Oh, you've got to sit awhile and watch me spin."

Yes, she is a skillful weaver,
And a slight of hand deceiver.
She is hoping that her web will suck you in.

Now, her thread's a little sticky,
And Matilda's not too picky.
If you take a peek she's lookin' kinda thin.

With her eight legs she will measure.
And she's thinkin' what a pleasure,
It would be to have you in between her skin.

If you're lookin' for a wife,
Why not save yourself some strife,
For Matilda's not the kind for marryin'.

And to her it does not matter.
All she wants to be is fatter.
She's a widow now,
and she will be again!

COATS

If I had to wear a coat,
I'd feel just like a fool.
There is no law against it,
And I would not break a rule.
My friends would think me weird,
So I'm not wearing one to school.
And if by chance I freeze to death,
At least I will look cool.

DEAD TORTOISE

I found a dead tortoise,
That has rigor mortis.
He's stiff as a boardise,
It's something to see.

He smells like a sewer,
Somewhat like manure.
It's causing a pewer
I think you'll agree.

No one will believe it,
If I don't retrieve it.
But I'd better leave it,
Or mom will kill me!

FANNY BABOON

Oh say have you heard about Fanny Baboon,
Who floated away on my brother's balloon?
They're telling me if all goes well pretty soon,
Should she keep on her course, she will land on the moon.

IN PUBLIC

When you are in public there's things you can't do.
Burps and gross noises are simply taboo.
There's just certain places that always get itches.
But Mom says to keep my hands out of my britches!

So here I am dressed in my very best clothes.
Can't scratch where it itches, I can't pick my nose.
The torture I feel now does not have a match.
I think I will die if I can't burp and scratch.

GIRLS NEVER BURP

I've heard them laugh, and giggle,
And squeak, and scream, and slurp.
But there is none to tell me why
That girls never burp?

There must be something wrong with them
To miss out on such pleasure.
The sound that comes from deep inside
Is really quite a treasure.

You know us guys can do it
Just 'bout any time we choose.
But if a girl would make a burp,
It'd prob'ly hit the news.

My dog's a girl and she will burp
After every meal.
Since she can do it, girls should try,
And see how good they'd feel.

I asked a girl, "Why don't you burp?"
And then she clearly stated
That she could never ever burp.
She's too sophisticated!

I'm glad I wasn't born a girl.
That wouldn't have been fair.
I've heard they take a bath each night,
And wear clean underwear!

If a girl would like to learn a skill,
But can't find one to suit'er.
I could make her life complete,
And be her burping tutor!

JUNK FOOD

Carrot cake and apple pie,
Want to make it just for I.

Chocolate fudge and root beer float,
You'll get pudgy, start to bloat.

Greasy fries, banana splits,
Blur your eyes and give you zits.

Lemon tart and hot meat ball,
Give your heart cholesterol.

Clog my veins and arteries too,
Think I'll give it all to you!

LADYBUG

Ladybug, ladybug, are you a lady,
Or is there a chance you're a boy?
If you are a boy and I call you a lady,
I bet that can really annoy!

Ladybug, ladybug, if you're a lady,
I don't want to mess up your mind.
But if all your brothers and fathers were ladies,
That would soon end all ladybugkind!

So let's put the brakes on this stuff about ladies,
　　Yes, we must be politically right.
　　We've got to stop calling a boy bug a lady,
　　'Cause it just doesn't seem very bright.

　　　　Being a bug called a lady is rough,
　　　　For Michaels, and Jareds, and Gregs.
　　　　But others have lives that
　　　　are nearly as tough,
　　　　You can ask a girl daddy longlegs!

LOSING HAIR

At twelve I lost my hair.
It really wasn't fair!
But my dad, the barber, I menaced.
In time it grew back in,
And I got to thinkin'
I'm sure glad he wasn't a dentist!

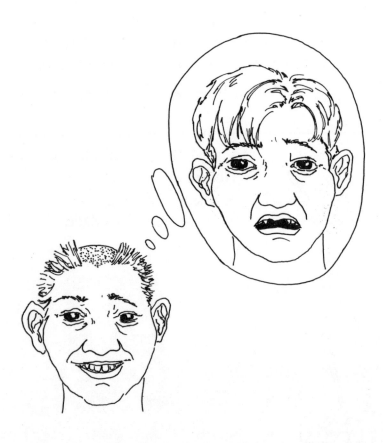

MARY'S PET

Mary had a little lamb,
It climbed up in a tree.
She was surprised when she found out,
It was a chimpanzee!

MY BROTHER, THE PAIN

One night my father and mother
Left me with my little brother.
He is a pain.
He will drive me insane.
He's ten times worse than any other.

He spilled his orange pop on the rugs.
He ate seven moths and two bugs.
Then he picked his nose,
Threw up on his clothes,
And then he ate
three giant slugs.

I'd like to get rid
of my brother.
That's what I told
Father and Mother.
They said if I would,
It won't do any good.
They would just go
and get me another.

MY CAR

My car, my car, where is my car?
I can not find it anywhar.
Not in the street or in the lot,
Or even in the family plot.
The lane, the road, the boulevard,
It's making my life much too hard.
I'm in a tiff. I'm in a quandary.
I could have left it in the laundry.
So, why do I make such a fuss?
For I forgot, I took the bus!

MY FRIEND THE BIRD

My friend the bird has had to live
Without the aid of laxative.
But nature did take care of that,
Or we'd hear thud, instead of splat!

OUTEY NOT AN INNEY

I have this problem, where should I begin?
When I discuss it people get all grinney,
For my belly button, it sticks out not in.
Yes, I have got an outey not an inney.

There are many questions on my mind.
I want some answers soon or I'll get pouty.
The hardest one that I can't seem to find,
Is which is best, an inney or outey?

My Dad told me his used to be an outey,
When he was young and also very thin.
He said he'd be elated and get rowdy,
If he were thin, and it stuck out again!

I'd rather have an inney that's my stance.
There isn't any
shadow of a doubt.
For my physique it
greatly would enhance,
To have my belly
button in, not out.

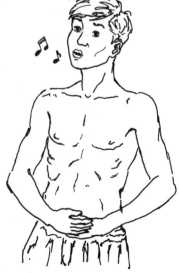

MY WISHES

I wish that I could drive a car.
I wish that I could fly a plane,
Go to a movie rated "R".
Being a kid is such a pain.

I'm always stuck in school all day.
The teachers make me learn the facts.
Ask all my friends, and they will say,
They're giving us all heart attacks!

I'm strong, I could stay out all night,
At least past twelve, or one, or two.
I'm old enough, it's just not right.
Grownups can't tell me what to do.

I'll just quit school, be free at last,
Do what I want and have some thrills,
Leave home and just forget my past,
But who is gonna pay my bills?

I sure don't want to get a job.
I am too young to work all day.
And I could never steal or rob,
Because I've learned crime doesn't pay.

I guess I'll go to school today.
    I'd hate to make my friends all sad.
        It sure beats working, I should say.
            Being a kid's not all that bad!

PENCIL SHARPENER

Why does the pencil sharp'ner
always gobble up my pencil?
This problem really bugs me, now.
It's getting more intensel.
I need to remedy it soon
or it will grow immensel.
I think I'll go mechanical,
that makes a lot more sensel.

PRUNES

I can tell you one thing now,
And you can turn me to a goon.
But there is no way any how
That I will ever eat a prune.

They are slimy. They are wrinkled.
They are gross, and they are brown.
Wouldn't eat them sugar sprinkled,
Rightside up or upside down!

My grandma eats them every day.
She says they are her plumber.
They affect her in a certain way,
And oh, that is a bummer.

You'll never catch me eatin' 'em.
Don't forget that's what I've told.
To eat one would be very dumb,
Unless, of course, you're old!

TIDDLYWINKS

Have you seen a tiddlywink?
What about a shuttlecock?
Words like these would make you think
Someone's brain's slipped off its rock.

Where would you a gaggle find?
Is it proper there to fard?
Kind of messes up your mind.
Do the questions seem too hard?

I have seen a tiddlywink,
A jumping plastic disk, oh my!
A shuttlecock's a birdie I think,
That will soar but cannot fly.

A gaggle flies, it isn't hard,
 A flock of geese at any pace.
 And shame at what you thought was fard!
It's only make-upping your face.

Where do you look for these first three?
They're up in the air a'darting.
But should you chance to look for me
I'll be at my mirror a'farding!

WARTS

Warts.
Big warts.
Ugly big warts.
Green ugly big warts.
Toad's green ugly big warts.
My toad's green ugly big warts.
Love my toad's green ugly big warts.
But I love you more than I love my toad's green ugly big
warts!

WASPS

I hate wasps,
And I can't think of
anything that rhymes with'em,
Therefore, please disregard this poem.

YELLOW LINE

Down the road there is a line.
A yellow line that's doin' fine.

From time to time it's not connected,
And every night it is reflected.

If it should go from one to two,
There are some things you cannot do.

The chicken crossed this yellow line,
And she was doin' mighty fine.

Then came a truck she did not spy.
Now she's a nugget, my, oh my!

ZITS

In sixth grade I bore my first zit,
And I was awful proud of it.
My teacher checked it out for me.
He was first to congratulate me.

Now I'm in the seventh grade.
I've had more zits, I am afraid.
Congratulations I don't want,
If zits grow on my back or front.

What is this upon my face?
Something there looks out of place.
It's turning red, oh what is it?
Oh my gosh, a giant zit!

What a time for this to be,
Everyone will stare at me.
In my plans this puts a dimple.
Now I've got a great big pimple.

Do I have to go to school?
Big red blobs are just not cool.
Kids are staring at my cheek.
They all want to take a peak.

Can't believe what I am seein'.
I'm the most watched human bein'.
The biggest zit in seventh grade
Makes celebrities, I'm afraid.

Fame is nice in any season.
I'd like it for some other reason.
So if a record you should hit,
I hope it's not a mega-zit!

INDEX

Glossary

ep·i·der·mis (ĕp'ĭ-dûr'mĭs) *n.* The outer, protective, layer of the skin that covers the dermis.

fard (färd) *n.* To apply or paint the face with makeup.

fil·i·bus·ter (fĭl'ə-bŭs'tər) *n.* The use of delaying tactics, such as long speeches and introduction of irrelevant information, to obstruct the passage of a bill in the house or senate.

gag·gle (găg'əl) *n.* A flock of geese.

in·cog·ni·to (ĭn'kŏg-nē'tō) *adv.* Having one's identity disguised or concealed.

in·com·plete (ĭn'kəm-plēt') *adj. Football.* A pass not caught or not caught in bounds: *an incomplete forward pass.*

mo·rass (mə-răs', mô-) *n.* Something that hinders, or overwhelms: *a morass of detail.*

rigor mor·tis (rĭg'ər môr'tĭs) *n.* Muscular stiffening occurring several hours after death.

shut·tle·cock (shŭt'l-kŏk') *n. Sports.* A small round flat ended piece of cork or rubber with a conical crown of feathers, used in badminton. Also known as a birdie.

so·phis·ti·cat·ed (sə-fĭs'tĭ-kā'tĭd) *adj.* Having acquired worldly knowledge or refinement; not simple or naïve.

spoon·er·ism (spōō'nə-rĭz'əm) *n.* [After Rev. William Archibald Spooner (1844-1930), of New College, Oxford, famous for such slips.] An interchange of sounds, usually initial sounds, of two or more words, especially a ludicrous one, such as *Let me sew you to your sheet* for *Let me show you to your seat.*

tid·dly·winks (tĭd'lē-wĭngks') *pl.n. Games.* Small plastic disk used in a game of the same name in which players try to snap the disks into a cup by pressing them on the edge with a larger one.

Acknowledgments

In "Filibuster," World Book is a registered trademark of World Book, Inc.

In "I'd Better Like Being a Kid," Bengay is a registered trademark of Pfizer, Inc.

"May I Have Your Attention," is based on an incident that actually happened to me when I was the teacher. The names have been changed to protect the innocent (and the guilty)!

In "School Food," back-tear-ia is from an old one liner.

In "Spoonerisms," slop you dripper is from Rindercella, a spoonerism story based on Cinderella.

Thank You

This book would not have been possible without the help of some special people. I especially want to thank JoAnn Jones, Anitra Steele and Craig Warner, along with Craig Piburn and Big Shoe Graphics, a student run ad agency on the campus of Northwest Missouri State University, Maryville, Missouri.

ABOUT THE AUTHOR

Steve Rideout has authored hundreds of humorous poems, but Don't Go Up A Windmill is his first book. He taught 5th, 6th, and 7th grades for nearly 17 years in the Kansas City area. Before leaving the teaching profession he shared some Ogden Nash poems with his students. That sparked his interest in writing humorous poetry. He now performs his poetry for audiences of all ages.

Mr. Rideout and his wife, both born and raised in Independence, Missouri, still live in the Kansas City Area. When their son and daughter are in college, thier dog soaks up most of the attention.

Photo by Tom Mitchell

ORDER FORM

Need more copies of Don 't Go Up A Windmill?

On a blank sheet of paper PRINT:

Please send me ___copy(ies) of Don't Go Up A Windmill.

Name (Please print or type)
Address
City
State
Zip
Telephone
Purchase Order Number (if necessary)
Amount enclosed

Enclose $9.95 for each copy plus $2.50 shipping and handling for the first book and $.75 for each additional book in the United States. Add $3.00 for books shipped to Canada. Allow four to eight weeks for delivery. Send check or money order payable to Blue Windmill Books. No cash or C.O.D.'s please. Prices subject to change without notice.
Quantity discounts available upon request.

Mail To:
Blue Windmill Books
PO Box 194
Blue Springs, MO 64013